Soccer Defending:

A Step-by-Step Guide on How to Stop the Other Team

Dylan Joseph

Soccer Defending: A Step-by-Step Guide on How to Stop the Other Team

By: Dylan Joseph

Bonus!

Wouldn't it be nice to have the steps in this book on an easy 1-page printout for you to take to the field? Well, here is your chance!

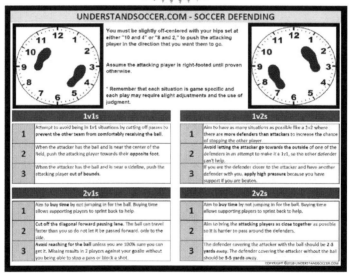

Go to this Link for an **Instant** 1-Page Printout: UnderstandSoccer.com/free-printout.

This FREE guide is simply a "Thank You" for purchasing this book. This 1-page printout will ensure that the knowledge you obtain from this book makes it to the field.

Table of Contents

About the Author

There I was, a soccer player who had difficulties scoring. I wanted to be the best on the field but lacked the confidence and know-how to make my goal a reality. Every day, I dreamed about improving, but the average coaching and my lack of knowledge only left me feeling alone and like I couldn't attain my goal. I was a quiet player and my performance often went unnoticed.

This all changed after my junior year on the Varsity soccer team of one of the largest high schools in the state. During the team and parent banquet at the end of the season, my coach decided to say something nice about each player. When it came to my turn to receive praise, the only thing he came up with was that I had scored two goals that season even though it was against a lousy team, so they didn't really count...

It was a very painful statement that after the 20+ game season, all that could be said of my efforts were two goals that didn't count. Since that moment, I have been forever changed considering one of my greatest fears came true; I was called out in front of my family and friends. Because of that, I got serious. With a new soccer mentor, I focused on the training necessary to obtain the skills to build my confidence and become the goal scorer I always dreamed of being. The next season, after just a few months, I found myself moved up to the starting position of center midfielder and scored my first goal of the 26 game season in only the third game.

I kept up the additional training led by a proven goal scorer to build my knowledge. Fast forward to present day and as a result of the work and focus on the necessary skills, I figured out how to become a goal scorer who averages about two goals and an assist per game, all because of an increase in my understanding of how to play soccer. With a new soccer mentor, I was able to take my game from bench-warmer who got called out in front of everybody to the most confident player on the field.

Currently, I am a soccer trainer in Michigan working for Next Level Training. I advanced through their rigorous program as a soccer player and was hired as a trainer. This program has allowed me to guide world-class soccer players for over a decade. I train soccer players in formats ranging from one-hour classes to weeklong camps and from instructing groups of 30 soccer players all the way down to working one-on-one with individuals looking to play for the United States National Team. If you live in the metropolitan Detroit area and want to be the best player in the league, Next Level Training is for you. Learn more at Next-LevelTraining.com. Please leave a review for this book at the end.

Additional Books by the Author that are Available on Amazon:

Soccer Shooting & Finishing
Soccer Dribbling & Foot Skills
Soccer Passing & Receiving

Dedication

This book is dedicated to the soccer players, coaches, and parents who are reading this book to improve their knowledge and to strengthen others around them. Whether it be for yourself, your team, or your child, growing to help others and yourself develop is exceptionally noble and speaks volumes to the person you are. Your time and effort spent will not go unnoticed.

Also, this book is dedicated to the content editors and grammar editors for the Understand Soccer Series. Specifically, these editors are Kimberly Stewart, Paul Marvar, Kevin Solorio, Toni Sinistaj, and Youssef Hodroj. These important editors have provided tremendous feedback to help with improving the examples in this book as well as the flow of the wording and sentence structures. Having an outstanding editing team as I do has really made it so you, the reader, do not have to focus on mistakes in the writing that take away from your ability to gain the knowledge revealed within these pages. I cannot thank these wonderful individuals enough.

Preface

This book was written to change the way players think about and play the game of soccer. I struggled for years with sub-average performances as a defender, defensive center midfielder, and outside midfielder. I was often placed in these positions because I could not score. Due to immaturity, I did not like others correcting my form since I knew it needed considerable improvement, so I would take it personally when someone gave me feedback. I realized that this was limiting my ability to become the player that I wanted to be.

Therefore, I sought out the knowledge that allowed me to score multiple goals a game, defend correctly, pass with excellent form, etc. As a result of this success, I could not help but share my understanding of the game to other players who are looking to improve, parents who want to boost their child's confidence on the field, and coaches who want to be viewed as outstanding by all of their players and their players' parents. Though I train players individually and in small groups, I know that writing the information down in a book will allow it to reach more eyes, build more confidence, and make a significant impact on the world.

Soccer is such a fun and exciting sport for some and I want it to be that way for all. I am a fan of learning from books and even YouTube videos on how to become better at soccer. I find, however, that there is typically no logical order on how the videos are created, so viewers of the video obtain bits and pieces of knowledge here and there, but do not understand the steps on how to put the pieces together. That is where this book comes in: To fill in those voids in the understanding of how to position your body as a defender, when to be aggressive, and the keys to winning 1v1s, 2v1s, 1v2s, and 2v2s.

This book dives deep into the important topics of soccer. Though the correct form and tactics are extremely helpful in ensuring the ball does not end up in your team's net, you also need a strong mindset to improve on any weaknesses, solidify your strengths, and implement many tips, tricks, tweaks, and techniques to become the person on your team that consistently dispossess the other team.

This book will help you become the most admired defender on your team. Understand that changing up one or two things may help you become better, but once you start implementing most, if not all of the techniques described in this book, you will see a significant improvement in your performance on the field. The knowledge in this book is only helpful when applied.

Therefore, apply it to be sure you are allowing 10X less goals each season, which will lead to several more wins every season for your team. For any words that you are unsure of the meaning, please reference the glossary in the back of the book.

INDIVIDUAL SOCCER PLAYER'S PYRAMID

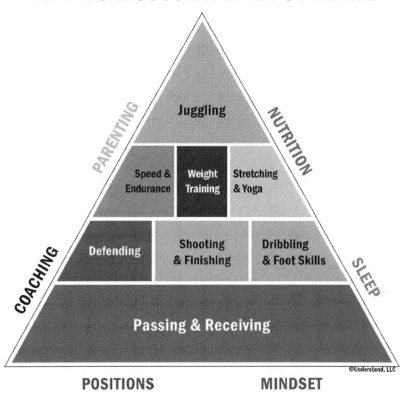

If you are looking to improve your skills, your child's confidence, or your players' abilities, it is essential to understand where this book fits into the bigger picture of developing a soccer player. In the image above, you can see that the most critical field-specific things to work on are at the base of the Individual Soccer Player's Pyramid. Note: A team's pyramid may look slightly different based on the tactics the players can handle and the approach the coach decides to use for games. The pyramid is a quality outline when you are looking to improve an individual soccer player's game. All of the elements in the pyramid and the items surrounding it play a meaningful part in becoming a better player, but certain things should be read and mastered first before moving on to other topics.

You will notice that passing & receiving is at the foundation of the pyramid because if you can receive a pass and make a pass in soccer, you will be a useful teammate. Though you may not be the one that is consistently scoring, the person that is dispossessing the other team, or the player that can dribble through several opponents, you will have the fundamental tools needed to play the sport and contribute to your team.

As you move one layer up, you find yourself with a decision to make on how to progress. Specifically, the pyramid is created with you in mind because each soccer player and each soccer position has different needs. Therefore, your choice regarding which path to take first is dictated by the position you play and more importantly, by the position that you want to play. In soccer and life, just because you are in a particular spot, position, or even a job, it does not mean that you have to stay there forever if that is not your choice. However, it is not recommended to refuse playing a position if you are not in the exact role you want. It takes time to develop the skills that will allow you to make a shift from one position to another.

If you are a forward or if you want to become one, then consider your route on the second layer of the pyramid to start with shooting & finishing. As your abilities to shoot increase, your coach will notice your new finishing skills and be more likely to move you up the field if you are not a forward already. Be sure to communicate to the coach that you desire to be moved up the field to a more offensive position, which will increase your chances as well. If you are already a forward, then dive deep into this topic to ensure you become the leading scorer on your team and in the entire league. Notice that shooting & finishing is considered less critical than passing & receiving because you have to pass the ball up the field before you can take a shot on net.

Otherwise, you can start by progressing to dribbling & foot skills from passing & receiving because the proper technique is crucial to dribble the ball well. It is often necessary for a soccer player to use a skill to protect the ball from the other team or to advance the ball up the field to place their team in a favorable situation to score. The selection of this route is often taken first by midfielders and occasionally by forwards.

Defending is another option of how you can proceed from passing & receiving. Being able to keep the other team off the scoreboard is not an easy task. Developing a defender's mindset, learning which way to push a forward, understanding how to position your body, knowing when to foul, and using the correct form for headers is critical to a defender on the back line looking to prevent goals.

Finish all three areas in the second layer of the pyramid before progressing up the pyramid. Dribbling and defending the ball (not just shooting) are useful for an attacker, shooting and defending (not just dribbling) are helpful for a midfielder, while shooting and dribbling (not just defending) are helpful for a defender. Having a well-rounded knowledge of the skills needed for the different positions is important for all soccer players. It is especially essential for those soccer players looking to change positions in the future. Shooting & finishing, dribbling & foot skills, and defending are oftentimes more beneficial for soccer players to learn first than the next tier of the pyramid, so focus on these before spending time on areas higher up in the pyramid. In addition, reading about each of these areas will help you to understand what your opponent wants to do as well.

Once you have improved your skills at the 1st and 2nd tiers of the pyramid, move upwards to fitness. As you practice everything below this category on the pyramid, your fitness and strength will naturally increase. It is difficult to go through a passing/dribbling/finishing drill for a few minutes without being out of breath. Performing the technical drills allows soccer players to increase their fitness naturally. This reduces the need to focus exclusively on running for fitness. Coming from a soccer player and trainer (someone with a view from both sides), I know that a constant focus on running is not as fulfilling and does not create long-lasting improvements.

Whereas, emphasizing the shooting capabilities, foot skills, and defending knowledge of a soccer player does create long-lasting change. Often, the coaches that focus on running their players in practice are the coaches that care to improve their team but have limited knowledge of many of the soccer-specific topics that would quickly increase their players' abilities. Not only does fitness in soccer include your endurance, but it also addresses your ability to run with agility and speed, develop strength and power, while improving your flexibility through stretching and yoga to become a well-rounded soccer player.

Similarly to the tier below it, you should focus on the fitness areas that will help you specifically, while keeping all of the topics in mind. For example, you may be a smaller soccer player that could use some size. Then, you would emphasize weight training and gain the muscle to avoid being pushed off the ball. However, you would still want to stretch before and after a lifting workout or soccer practice/game to ensure that you stay limber and flexible, so that you can recover quickly and avoid injuries.

Maybe you are a soccer player in your 20s, 30s, or 40s. Then, emphasizing your flexibility and practicing a bit of yoga would do a world of good to ensure you keep playing soccer for many more years. However, doing a few sets of push-ups, pull-ups, squats, lunges, sit-ups, etc. per week will help you maintain or gain a desirable physique.

Furthermore, you could be in the prime of your career in high school, college, or at a pro level, which would mean that obtaining the speed and endurance to run for 90+ minutes is the most essential key to continue pursuing your soccer aspirations.

Finally, we travel to the top of the pyramid, which includes juggling. Juggling the soccer ball is something fun to practice in your own free time away from the field or when you are standing in line and waiting to start a drill. It will certainly help with your first touch, but there are more important things to develop during an individual's or team's practice. A general recommendation is that when you can juggle the ball 50 times in a row or more with either of your feet, continuing to work on juggling will not provide huge increases in your performance. Therefore, use juggling as a way to fill otherwise unproductive time in training or during free time to more quickly become a great soccer player. The importance of juggling is explained in more detail in the first book of the series - *Soccer Training: A Step-by-Step Guide on 14 Topics for Intelligent Soccer Players, Coaches, and Parents*, in addition to a host of other critical topics you need to know as a soccer player, coach, or parent.

If you have not read *Soccer Training: A Step-by-Step Guide*, it is highly recommended that you do to gain general knowledge of the crucial topics within the areas of the pyramid. Furthermore, there are a few soccer terms that are described in detail in the *Soccer Training* book that may only be referenced in this book. Picking up a copy of the book will act as a good gauge to see how much you know about each topic. This will help to determine if a book later in the series written about a specific subject in the soccer pyramid will be beneficial for you.

The last portion of the pyramid are the areas that surround the pyramid. Though these are not skills and topics that can be addressed by your physical abilities, they each play key roles in rounding out a complete soccer player. For example, having a supportive parent/guardian or two is beneficial for transporting the child to games, providing the equipment needed, the fees for the team, expenses for individual training, and encouragement. Having a quality coach will help the individual learn how their performance and skills fit into the team's big picture.

Sleeping enough is critical to having energy in practices and on game days, in addition to recovering from training and games. Appropriate soccer nutrition will increase the energy and endurance of a soccer player, help the soccer player achieve the ideal physique, and significantly aid in the recovery of the athlete. Understanding soccer positions will help to determine if a specific role is well-suited given your skills. It is important to know that there are additional types of specific positions, not just forwards, midfielders, and defenders. A former or current professional player in the same position as yours can provide you guidance on the requirements of effectively playing that position.

Last, but not least, is developing a mindset that leaves you unshakable. This mindset will help you become prepared for game situations, learn how to deal with other players, and be mentally tough enough to not worry about circumstances that you cannot control, such as the type of field you play on, the officiating, or the weather. The pyramid is a great visual aid to consider when choosing what areas to read next as a soccer player, coach, or parent. Now that you understand where this book plays into the overall picture, let us begin.

Chapter 1

The Main Thing is to Keep the Main Thing the Main Thing

The game is on the line with only 30 seconds to go and the score is tied. You, a defender, take a shot from the 30-yard line and it is a fantastic upper-90 goal to win the game for your team. The fans cheer, your team celebrates your accomplishment, and you feel on top of the world. This story is just that, a story. It is something that is great when it happens, but as a defender, it should not be how you judge your performance. What separates good defenders from great defenders is game intelligence. Therefore, let us review some high-level concepts that all defenders should understand:

1. Your biggest priority is to prevent goals
2. Avoid dribbling in most circumstances
3. Stay positive
4. A small touch goes a long way
5. Hands wide outside your 18-yard box and hands behind you inside it

1. **Your most significant objective as a defender is to keep the other team from scoring.** Not to score, not to dazzle the fans with your foot skills, but to prevent the

other team from scoring. Therefore, it is okay to clear the ball up the field when you are under extreme pressure inside your 18-yard box. It is okay for you to pass the ball off to the midfielders and forwards to let them do their jobs of providing goals for your team. It is okay for you not to be on the stat sheet for a goal or an assist.

2. **Often, avoid dribbling as a defender.** Look for passes and sometimes clearances. Soccer is a probability game and if you lose the ball, the forward on the other team will have fewer people to beat than if the ball started at the opposition's defense. Remember, a defender is 90% judged by the number of goals scored against them and not by the flair of their dribbling abilities. However, understand the defensive role on your team. The right outside defender or left outside defender may play as wingbacks where they are expected to dribble the ball up the field and cross it into the box.

3. **Do not forget about the good things you do.** I get it... defending is tough. You are constantly throwing your body on the line for your team with minimal recognition. Let us face it, people often only notice defenders when they mess up and the forwards are usually the ones grabbing the glory on most soccer teams. Accept that this is a reality and develop the mindset that it is most important to win as a team and not as an individual.

4. **Most times, all you need is to touch the ball slightly.** Too many defenders feel that if they have not entirely dispossessed the attacker and played the ball to a teammate, they have not successfully performed their job. Making contact, even with just a toe, will often mess up the attacking player's plan and prevent the ball from going in your net. As players on the other team are attacking against you, they create plans of attack to score. Just a simple and slight redirection of the ball, while they are attempting to carry out their plan, will often be more than enough to slow or completely stop the other team's forward progress.

5. **Allow your hands to be in a natural position outside of your 18-yard box and keep them clasped behind you when you are inside your 18-yard box and the other team has the ball.** Similar to the last point, a small touch on the ball will often stop an attacker's progress, as will a nudge with your arm. As a defender, it is crucial that you play bigger than you are. The easiest way to do this is to keep your arms away from your body to make it more difficult for the player attacking to dribble around you. Additionally, this creates a bigger appearance for you that will slightly reduce the attacker's confidence of dribbling past you. If you are outside of your 18-yard box, having your arms up and your forearm against the attacker as they

are receiving the ball is a phenomenal way to increase the difficulty of their first touch. Disrupting their first touch will help to limit additional moves after that if they cannot gain control of the ball.

Additionally, if the attacker is pushing the ball past you while they are dribbling, do not be afraid to extend your arms in front of the opponent to help prevent them from beating you to the ball. From a young age, soccer players are often taught that you must keep your hands perfectly by your side. As you begin to play at higher levels, most referees do not call players with their arms extended. **Play with a big presence** unless you are in your 18-yard box. In these instances, keeping your hands clasped behind you is important. If, while you are attempting to block a shot or cross, the ball deflects off of one of your arms, you will give the other team the easiest opportunity to score, which is a penalty kick. When watching professional soccer games, you will often notice that just one minor mistake by a defender in their own 18-yard box, often decides the outcome of a game. An accidental handball allows the other team an uncontested shot on net from the penalty spot. This type of mental mistake is one of the easiest ways to destroy your team's momentum and lose your teammates' confidence in you.

Again, the main thing is to keep the main thing the main thing. As a defender, your primary role is to keep the ball out of your team's net. Many of the things we have briefly discussed here will be further expanded upon in chapters to come. These concepts are great insights that every quality defender implements into their game.

Chapter 2

Reading the Game & Playing Each Player Differently

Defenders are judged on many things. As mentioned in the first chapter, the most important thing for the entire defense is preventing the other team from scoring. However, goals allowed does not make the best measurement of a defender's effectiveness, since one mistake from a defender other than yourself could result in a goal. Therefore, there are additional ways to track a defender's abilities by using metrics like:

1. Recoveries
2. Interceptions
3. Blocks
4. Clearances

These metrics are listed in their order of importance. Recoveries are when a defender regains possession of the ball shortly after your team was dispossessed. **Recoveries are important because the best time to regain possession is within six seconds after it is stolen**, according to Pep Guardiola the former player who is one of the most successful coaches in the world. His methodology is to recover the ball with a six-second burst of high-intensity pressing. Often, the turnover occurs in the other team's half, so the press is performed by the forwards and midfielders. Having forwards and midfielders press the other team for the ball is known as high-pressing and doing it throughout the game takes considerable energy away from the forwards and midfielders who are responsible for scoring. This is why Guardiola tells his players to high-press for roughly six seconds and then to assume a standard defensive formation that takes less energy. All the players nearest the ball are required to rush towards the individual in possession while the rest of the team moves closer together for a tighter defensive formation. The close players shut down passing options and attempt to force an immediate mistake. If no error occurs, the tight positioning is the basis for a great defensive formation.

Reading the game is vital because intercepting a pass displays a superior soccer intellect. It shows the defender's ability to anticipate, which is a critical aspect of an intelligent soccer player. A defender that can anticipate waits until the perfect time to step into a passing lane and intercept or deflect a pass. Another important aspect of intercepting a pass is positioning. To be correctly positioned demonstrates an understanding of how a play develops in a game. Being in the right place at the right time requires familiarity with both your team's tactics and the other team's game plan.

For positioning, a good general rule of thumb is to stay between the attacking player and the goalie. Cutting off the attackers' angle to the net makes it easier to block shots. If an attacker gets past you on a wing, typically the best line to recover is along a straight line between you and the near post. If the attacker strays out of that line, hopefully, it will take them near another defender on your team. If the defensive players on your team are getting beat regularly, many teams will switch to a formation in which most of the team is behind the ball, a strategy known as "parking the bus."

Next, people are different. While defending against attacking players on the opposing team, identify their strengths and weaknesses. It is essential to exploit the weaknesses and diminish the forwards' ability to use their strengths:

1. Watch them in warm-ups/watch them in other games
2. Communicate to your other defenders on how you intend to defend the forward
3. Change your plan, if needed

1. Though it takes more time to scout the other team, it can pay off substantially. **Without having seen a team or a player before, you may make assumptions based on**

how they look and this can be detrimental. Assuming results in you expecting that the taller players will be on the end of headers, all the team's opposing players are right-footed, etc.

2. **Let your teammates know your intentions for defending attackers on the other team.** Communicating this will allow you to hear their thoughts too and ensure the entire back line is on the same page.

3. **If you realize that your defensive plan is not working, then change the plan.** Whether it be 15 minutes into the game or at halftime, change your plan to include the newly discovered information based on what you have learned so far playing against the other team.

Remember that each player on both teams has their own strengths and weaknesses. The more time spent learning about the other team, communicating what you have learned, and developing a plan with your teammates, the easier it will be to keep the other team off the scoreboard. The hardest working players both on and off the field often are the best or are on their way to becoming the best soccer players.

Chapter 3

Body Positioning and the 1v1

As a defender, you want your body positioning to be angled. You never want to have your hips pointed ("squared") at the attacker completely because then it allows the attacker to go to the right of you, to the left of you, and between your legs. **You want to be angled, but not entirely turned to the side.** Position one of your sides so it faces the attacker, but still at a diagonal. If your feet were hands on a clock, you would want your feet positioned at either "10 and 4," as shown in the first image or "8 and 2," as shown in the second image.

This body positioning allows you to push them either to the left or the right. Standing at "10 and 4" would push them to their left foot and standing at "8 and 2" would push them to their right foot. Keep in mind that just standing directly in front of them and turning your hips will not force them in the direction that you want them to go. **You must be slightly off-centered with your hips set at either "10 and 4" or "8 and 2," to push them in the direction that you want them to go.**

If you just turn your hips directly in front of a good dribbler, they will attack the side that you are not facing, all other things being equal, to make it easier for them to get around you. This forces you to turn farther to pursue them. Therefore, it is best to position yourself slightly closer to the side you do not want them to go. If they attack in the direction you are forcing them, your positioning will make it easier for you to tackle or pursue.

As a defender, it is essential you are active by being on your toes. You do not want to be caught standing still. You want to be in a low stance, bent at the knees, and bent at the hips. Being on your toes will allow you to accelerate faster when the attacker does a skill and tries to sprint away. As discussed in *Soccer Shooting & Finishing: A Step-by-Step Guide on How to Score*, great coaches and trainers will teach their soccer players the following three things while they are developing their skills to perform in 1v1 situations:

1. Use a foot skill.
2. Attack with speed.
3. Aim to use your dominant foot to shoot.

A defender must be able to understand what the other team's player with the ball is aiming to do in the 1v1 scenario. Learning their go-to tactics allows you to develop a plan to stop them. **First, the attacker will be looking to use a foot skill.** Use of a foot skill such as a jab or a scissor may cause you to turn your body in the wrong direction, making it easier for the attacker to go past you. As a defender trying to prevent their foot skill, address the situation even before the attacker obtains the ball. By applying significant pressure to them and stopping the attacker from receiving a pass, you do not even need to worry about the opponent performing a foot skill. However, should they receive the ball, watch the direction of their hips when performing the foot skill. Understand that a highly skilled attacker will misleadingly turn their hips in the direction they want you, the defender, to go. Luckily, most attackers are not experienced or knowledgeable enough and often show their true intentions with their hips.

Next, the forward wants to attack with speed. The acceleration after the foot skill is critical for the forward to create the space and separation from you. As a result, you must look to interfere with their ability to accelerate. The best way to do this when they have successfully performed a foot skill is to extend your arms in front of the direction they are looking to go. Aim to slow them or even nudge them as they are taking their next touch to force a mistake. Do not merely let them past you without doing everything in your power to prevent it.

Lastly, whenever you defend in a 1v1 situation, one of the main goals of the attacker is to take a shot with their dominant foot. **Obviously, the foot they are more comfortable using will provide a more accurate and powerful shot compared to a shot with their opposite foot.** In a 1v1, a good striker will attempt to go in the direction they desire. However, a great defender will prevent them from going to their dominant foot. Therefore, not only is being at "10 and 4" or "8 and 2" important but standing slightly off-center to force the attacker to their opposite foot is necessary too.

In a 1v1 game situation, where you push the defender depends on the portion of the field they are on and their location relative to your teammates. Ideally, if you were in the middle of the field, you would want to push the attacker to their weak foot. How do you know which foot is there weak foot? **Always assume it is their left foot until you observe otherwise.** However, when you are along a sideline and it is still a one versus one, you want to position your body in a way that will push them out of bounds and towards the sideline. Notice in the image that the defender is slightly to the attacker's right side, which will more often than not force the attacker to their left.

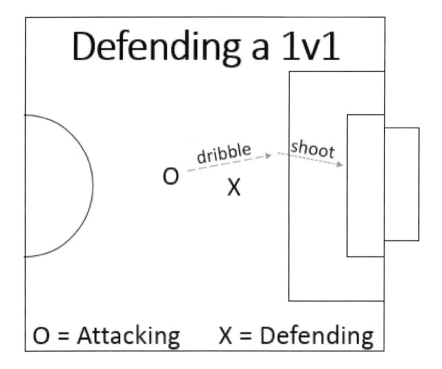

At Next Level Training (NLT), the premier soccer training company in Michigan, we hired another trainer who happens to have the same name as me. Sure enough, a few months later, we both ended up playing against each other in a league match. Keep in mind that this other Dylan is a great guy and an excellent addition to our NLT staff. However, I was playing an attacking midfield position in the game and at times was defending against him.

As described previously, I followed the rule and forced him to his left foot when he had the ball. I soon found out that this was to his advantage as he was left-footed. He struck a wonderful shot that barely missed the net, but I took a mental note of this for future use in the game. I ended up defending him several more times that game and because I now knew that he was left-footed, I gave him much more space to his right foot. This tactic worked well for the rest of the game and he was unable to take another shot while I was defending him. Sadly, some of my teammates did not take the advice to push him to his opposite foot and he ended up scoring two goals against us because they let him use his dominant foot.

To conclude, your objectives when defending in a 1v1 are to first prevent the defender from receiving the ball by applying pressure on them. Next, if they receive the ball, watch out for a foot skill by focusing on their hips, while directing them to their opposite foot using a slightly off-center stance. If they successfully perform a foot skill, then use your arms by placing them in front of the attacker to slow their speed as they aim to accelerate past you. Check out the third book in the Understand Soccer Series, *Soccer Dribbling & Foot Skills: A Step-by-Step Guide on How to Dribble Past the Other Team*, for various foot skills that trained attackers will use when attempting to dribble around you. Obtaining the knowledge that your opponent has will make it easier for you to learn how to stop them.

Chapter 4

Being Physical and When to Foul

As previously mentioned in this book, one of the best ways to be physical is to extend your arms in front of the attacking player to slow them down. **In a game, the referee will hardly ever call a foul on you if your arms are up and against an opponent.** The trick here is to not grab them or have your hands on them. At a young age, they teach you to keep your arms by your side. However, if the referee is not going to call your arms being up in a game, then use this to your advantage.

Extend your elbow and your shoulder to engage with them. It is crucial that you make yourself look bigger because it makes it harder for the opposing player to travel around you. Having your arms up will make it easier for you to place your forearm against their body and use your shoulder muscle to keep them away from the ball. When you watch professional defenders, they tend to use their hands and arms a lot because, in most situations, the referee will not call anything against them.

As a defender, you will often find yourself as the only player left between the attacker and an easy shot on your goalkeeper. Therefore, it is essential to know when to lunge for the ball and when to continue to backpedal while expecting your teammates to sprint back in order to help stop the person attacking. As a rule of thumb, if it is a 1v1 situation with just you standing between the attacker and the goal, then backpedal to wait for an opportunity to block their shot while also attempting to push them towards a sideline with your body positioning. Unless you are 100% sure that if you lunge for the ball, you will succeed in kicking it away or taking possession, you should avoid lunging in for the ball. **This is key because if you miss**

the ball, the attacker will quickly dribble around you and have a breakaway against the keeper.

When jockeying (backpedaling and keeping the defender in front of you), your momentum is going in the same direction as the attacker. Both bodies are moving towards your own goal. **However, lunging/reaching in for the ball changes your body's momentum from going backward to going forward.** Changing your momentum is significant because if you miss the ball, you will need to come to a complete stop and then need to start running again hoping that you can quickly accelerate to a sprint and recover from your mistake. This rarely happens; instead, the attacker takes an easy shot during their breakaway. Therefore, in 1v1 situations, look to react based on the attacker's move. If they attempt to shoot the ball, make sure you block it. If they try to dribble, force them to their weak foot and push them towards the sideline to decrease the angle they have to approach the net.

However, when you have more teammates alongside you and behind you, it is appropriate to reach in for the ball because even if you miss, your teammates will support you and help to cover for your mistake. In this case, lunging in with the intention to steal the ball is an acceptable risk that can start a counterattack while the other team's defense has not yet established their shape to defend properly. Remember that this is a general rule and specific situations will differ. Therefore, it is necessary to develop both your skills and ability to judge the situation.

In soccer, there are certain instances when it is acceptable to foul, although it is never advisable to tell someone to hurt an opposing player intentionally. **A tactical foul is appropriate when your team is slow to get back to defend and the other team has more attackers than your team has defenders behind the ball.** In this instance, a tactical foul to stop the play may be appropriate. Though yellow cards are not fun to obtain, in reality, they are just a warning. Simply holding a player or extending your leg too far out when the attacker is dribbling can create the time needed for your team to position more players between the ball and the net.

In conclusion, use your arms to slow your opponent down and consider making a necessary tactical foul. Avoid lunging in for the ball when you do not have teammates to help, but be sure to attempt to steal the ball when you have plenty of supporting teammates behind you. Be physical and use your judgment while defending to determine what works best in each situation for you. Understand that there are times to commit to stealing the ball and times to wait for the attacker to act. The better the attacker, the more you should respect their foot skills and position yourself to avoid being outskilled by them. Vincent Kompany and Pepe are great examples of defenders who are very physical and use their aggressiveness to their advantage.

Chapter 5

Heading the Ball

Heading the ball is a skill to be mastered by all soccer players, but is especially vital for defenders attempting to prevent the other team from scoring. Since this book focuses on defending, this chapter will emphasize heading the ball to stop the other team from scoring.

First, when performing a header in soccer, it is essential you contract your body forward by pulling your arms backward. **Contracting your body, in addition to your neck, allows you to snap your body forward to accelerate your head quickly towards the ball, which**

will dramatically increase the power of your headers. Make sure to head through the ball to ensure even more power and most importantly, more accuracy. This portion of heading is easily learned, but being able to judge the flight of the ball to time your jump appropriately takes practice and experience.

Whether you are a 5'5" defender or a 6'5" defender, you should practice your ability to clear the ball using your head. **When doing a header, use your forehead, not the top of your head, to be more accurate with your headers.** However, to deflect the ball when it is being crossed, it is appropriate to use the top of your head too if you cannot make contact with the ball using your forehead. It is tough to be accurate when the top of the head is used because your eyes are off the ball for a significant amount of time. To ensure accuracy on your headers, you must keep your eyes open until a split second before the ball hits your head.

The two most common defensive tactics during a corner kick are to man-mark players or to have each defender and midfielder cover a zone. Whether you are man-marking or covering a zone, looking where players of the other team are located allows you to know in which direction you should clear the ball.

Being able to use good judgment in soccer differentiates good defenders from great defenders. Great defenders are concerned with doing what it takes for their team to win. A great player knows deep down that their team's success will bring them more recognition in the long run anyway. When a forward is attempting a header, if they are farther away than the penalty spot, avoid contact with them, as it is very unlikely that their header will have enough pace on it to travel past a goalkeeper. However, if the forward is in the 6-yard box, then make sure you at least are making contact with the forward to disrupt their ability to head the ball if you cannot head the ball away yourself.

During a corner kick, forwards are constantly moving to evade you. Often, forwards recruit other teammates to set picks and obstruct your path. Therefore, make sure to communicate when you need help. Aim to avoid forwards traveling into your blind spot where you have to choose between viewing the ball or seeing the attacker.

Conversely, when your team is attacking and on the other team's half, your ability to head the ball is important to ensure that you can push the ball up the field and continue your team's attack. One way to overwhelm another team is to head any clearances back towards their net to continually attack. To do this effectively, you must be 100% certain that you can head the ball back into play. **Avoid going for the header if you are the last player on the back line of your team.** Forwards that know they are unlikely to win a header, will play the ball hoping it will go over your head and that they will have easy access to the net. Shorter players, like 5'7" Lionel Messi, do not attempt many headers due to their stature but look for defenders to misjudge a header and give them an easy scoring opportunity.

In summary, be sure to contract your whole upper body to hit the ball harder with your head than if you only contracted your head at the neck. Too many soccer players, myself included at times, will allow the ball to hit them in the head and then based on where their head is positioned, the ball will deflect softly towards the net or be a pass to a teammate. **Not extending at the neck creates weak headers which can be easily fixed by using the entire body to have a much more powerful header.**

Chapter 6

Defending in a 2v1

When there is a 2v1 and you are the only defender against two attacking players, there are several helpful guidelines to follow to increase your chances of preventing the other team from scoring or even shooting, as follows:

1. Aim to slow the speed of play as much as possible
2. Block the diagonally forward passing lane
3. Use your efforts towards stopping the person with the ball

Your first thought when you are the only defender in a 2v1 should be to slow the play down as much as possible to allow teammates to sprint back and provide support. Since a 2v1 does not give you many options, your best bet of slowing the speed of play down is to keep considerable space, at least 5 yards, between you and the attackers while you are outside your 18-yard box. **Reducing the space between you and the attacking player with the ball will force the attacker to either do a foot skill and sprint by you or to pass the ball diagonally forward so their teammate can run to the ball. Either of these options will speed up the play, which is exactly what**

you want to avoid. Considering that your primary aim is to keep the ball out of your net, you do not necessarily need to be the person that regains possession of the ball if you can buy time for a teammate to come back to do it with more favorable odds. Remember that the defensive objective of preventing the other team from scoring is more important than you receiving glory for a spectacular play.

A 2v1 when you are the only defender places you at a huge disadvantage and you must decide whether to attempt to shut down the person with the ball or to cut off the passing lane. Understand that this is very situational and each 2v1 will look slightly different. In general, you should aim to shut down the player with the ball while blocking the diagonally forward passing lane. **A horizontal pass on the field from one striker to the other is excellent for you, as the defender, because the ball is not advancing up the field with this pass, which provides an additional second or two for your supporting teammates to travel back towards the play.**

Defending a 2v1

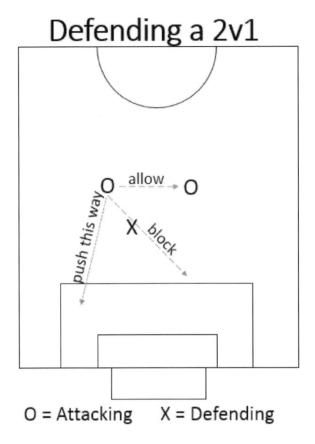

O = Attacking   X = Defending

Next, your primary focus should be on the person with the ball. Attempt to push them towards the end line to decrease their angle towards the net if they decide to shoot. Notice that in the image, the defender is not directly in front of the attacker but cutting off the diagonally forward passing lane and giving the defender some space to attack along the sideline without using their teammates help. **In essence, your goal should be to make the 2v1 a 1v1 by positioning yourself in a way that takes the other attacker out of the play.** The priority is to focus on shutting down the person with the ball.

The worst thing you can do in this situation is to reach in for the ball, miss it, and allow for an easy breakaway for two players on the other team. This will nearly always end up in the back of the net because the goalie must then position themselves to stop the person with the ball, but a simple pass to the other player will leave the entire net wide open for an easy tap-in goal.

In conclusion, always aim first to slow the speed of play, cut off the diagonally forward passing lane, and place the majority of your focus on the attacker with the ball. Work to make the 2v1 a 1v1 while providing time for teammates to travel back into position. Avoid reaching/lunging in for the ball unless you know with 100% certainty that you will dispossess the attacker or risk the terrible situation for your goalie of a two-person breakaway.

Chapter 7

Slide Tackling

As a soccer player, slide tackling may or may not be allowed in your league. Certain younger and non-competitive leagues will have rules against slide tackling. Therefore, make sure you are allowed to slide tackle before implementing any of the recommendations in this chapter.

First, consider a quote by Paolo Maldini, a left back and central defender for A.C. Milan and the Italian national team. Maldini is regarded as one of the best defenders of all time and only averaged one tackle every two games. **He states that "if I have to make a tackle then I have already made a mistake."** Even Xabi Alonso, the former Liverpool, Real Madrid, and Bayern Munich holding midfielder states that "I don't think tackling is a quality. It is something you have to resort to, not a characteristic of your game." Therefore, he makes an excellent point that slide tackling should be a last resort tactic. Slide tackling results from a soccer player who was caught out of place and is making a last-ditch effort to recover the ball.

Slide tackling wears and tears on your body and can cause an injury to the other player too, which

should always be avoided. Do not be a player that intends to hurt others. Just look at Sergio Ramos who caused the entire nation of Egypt and the Liverpool fan base to dislike him because of his aggressive tackle against Mohamed Salah a few weeks before the 2018 World Cup. Though this was not a slide tackle, it involved Ramos causing a shoulder injury that forced Liverpool's EPL record holder of 32 goals to leave before halftime and not return.

If you aim to have slide tackling as part of your defensive game, the appropriate gear helps tremendously. **Soccer sliders are basically underpants with padding to prevent your legs from being torn up when sliding.** If you slide on turf or inadequate grass fields, you will probably create a "strawberry" on your thigh. A strawberry (also known as a raspberry or road rash) is a friction burn on the skin of your hip/upper leg from slide tackling. Turf fields are the biggest culprits for strawberries and soccer sliders can help prevent these. Though sliders are helpful on grass fields, they are not as necessary, but still can help reduce physical injuries from slide tackling.

Next, commit to slide tackling when you are 100% certain that you will touch the ball before making contact with the other player. It will almost certainly be a yellow card or a red card if your slide tackle is from behind and prevents the other team from a chance at scoring. Therefore, when you slide tackle, aim to either trap the ball between your toes and shin so you can quickly attack in the other direction or strike it with the bone of your foot, where the leather meets the laces, to boot the ball either to a teammate or out of bounds. During a slide tackle, you are committing to going to the ground, which takes some time to stand up from and travel back into position. Therefore, slide tackling and having the ball still roll to the other team will surely catch you out of position.

Lastly, the principal thing when performing a slide tackle is to be traveling fast enough to slide across the grass effectively. **Therefore, slide tackling requires you to be running at full speed and slide foot first to dispossess the other team or block their shot.** Jogging and then attempting to slide tackle will most likely not get the job done.

In summary, consider the following when determining if you should slide tackle:

1. Avoid it in most situations and use it as a last resort
2. Use sliders under your shorts to prevent physical injuries
3. Slide when you are 100% sure you will touch the ball first
4. Travel fast enough to slide tackle effectively

Chapter 8

Reading the Attacking Player's Foot Skills

Understand that a well-executed move does not have any tells that make it easy for you to know what the person with the ball will do. Sometimes, you will simply be beaten by an effective skill, but reading the other player's body language will help ensure these situations are few and far between. Reading an attacker's foot skill implies that you are waiting for the attacker to act so that you may react. **A defender that aims to react is one that prefers to block shots, wait for the attacker to make a mistake, and dispossess an attacker when they attempt to perform a foot skill.** The other type of defender is one who looks to prevent the attacker from receiving the ball and is continually reaching in to attempt to gain possession of the ball. You should be able to recognize the following foot skills to help stop an attacking player:

1. Shot Fake
2. Jab or Scissor
3. Self-Pass or Roll

1. To determine if an attacking player is faking a shot or taking a shot, consider a few things. **For an actual shot, a**

player's arms go up, their leg contracts far behind their body, and they likely look at the net before they shoot (although not all players striking the ball will look at the net before shooting). Look at the attacker's shooting form in warm-ups to recognize their shooting style. Yes, this takes more time but can save you from not knowing how to defend your attacker at the start of a game.

2. Being able to know when the attacker is performing a scissor or a jab is a necessary skill for the reactive defender who waits for the attacker to act so they may react. In a poorly executed jab or scissor, the ball will often start directly in front of the attacker rather than with the ball to one side or the other as it should correctly begin. More importantly, the attacker should turn their hips toward the direction they want to fake you into thinking they are going. **However, a poorly executed jab or scissor is one where the attacker did not turn their shoulders or hips to fake you into believing they are going in one direction.** Therefore, the attacker's legs are showing they are faking one way, but their upper body is telling you a different story.

3. For a self-pass or a roll, you cannot read into the attacker's actions because these are skills that are performed only after you have over-committed and lunged in for the ball. These skills are the attacker's reaction to the

defender's action. **Therefore, lunging in for the ball is not often recommended unless you are 100% certain you will dispossess the attacker or if you have many players behind you to recover if the attacker speeds past after you miss dispossessing them.**

In conclusion, look for differences between a shot fake and the shot of a player to better tell when they are looking to use a foot skill versus when they plan to shoot. **One more thing not mentioned previously is that most players' legs will not travel all the way back when they fake a shot.** They will bend at the knee but will not bend at the hip. They can still generate some power using a windup like this, but most shots involve a full windup and not just a modest bend at the knee. Additionally, an attacker's body will point in the direction they intend to travel. Some defenders bait the attacker by intentionally showing the defender they will do one thing, such as leave a lane open for the attacker to dribble or pass the ball, but close it down at the last second. In each situation, determine if being a defender first to act is better or if you should react based on the attacker's moves.

Chapter 9

Defending in a 1v2

When taking on a single attacker and you are one of two defenders, it is critical that you look to make it as easy as possible for you and your teammate to prevent the attacker from scoring. Ask yourself how best can I stop the attacker and regain possession of the ball to start a counterattack?

A good striker will travel to the outside slightly where they only need to beat one defender to shoot the ball. Conversely, a good defender will force the attacker into their supporting teammate. To do this, all it takes is correct positioning in relation to the attacker. You do not want to position yourself directly in front of the attacker, but slightly off to the side so the attacker has an easier route by you on one side. However, that should be the side where your supporting defender is. See the following image for an example.

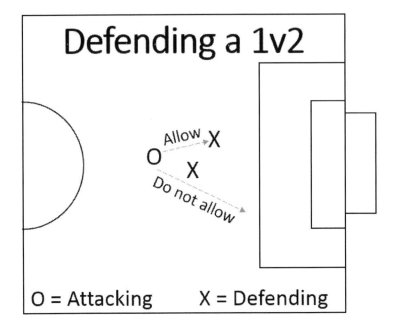

Notice that the first defender is forcing the attacker toward his or her teammate. This is good advice for a 1v3 when you are defending an attacker with two additional teammates. **The overarching goal is to have a more favorable advantage that the 1v2 provides over a 1v1 for your team when you are defending.** Aim to force the attacking player to take on all the defenders before they can shoot. In these instances, when you have more players, you do not want to wait for the attacker's teammates to come to support the player. Therefore, be aggressive and speed the pace of the play up to dispossess the attacker as quickly as possible.

Additionally, the abilities of the attacking player make a huge difference. Assess their strengths and determine how closely you should defend the attacker. When you have more defenders working against the sole player attacking, you want to be aggressive, but leave 2-3 yards of space between you and the attacker when they are great dribblers. Giving a bit of space makes it more difficult for the attacker to use a foot skill to accelerate past you and the other defender. However, if the attacker's strength is their ability to shoot, then you do not want to be any farther than 1-2 yards from them. You want to dispossess the attacker without giving them the space to take a shot.

In conclusion, make an attacker in a 1v2 beat both defenders by positioning your body so that they are pushed towards your teammate. Speed up the play while you have more players because you do not want additional opposing attackers to have time to support their teammate. Furthermore, assess the attacker's foot skills and shooting ability. Provide a yard or two more of space if they are a better dribbler than shooter.

Chapter 10

Defending Against Fast Restarts

Restarts are where the ball has gone out of bounds or has been awarded to a team because of a foul. The ball must be sent back into play for the game to continue. Restarts are a perfect opportunity for your opponent to catch your team off guard. More than likely, your team will take a few seconds to travel to the correct positions to defend the ball coming back into play. Frequently, defending teams will not be hustling hard enough to be in position during a restart. They may need to catch their breath or take a few seconds for a mental break. **If the other team quickly places the ball back into play for a "fast restart," it can create a quick disadvantage for your team.**

As an example, I use fast restarts to my advantage on offense during a corner kick. I will run as fast as I can to grab the ball, place the ball on the quarter circle near the flag, and then immediately look for a teammate who is making a delayed run into the box or is open and checking to the corner flag. A quick corner kick is useful because the defense is likely not set up optimally to defend and many will not be looking at the ball initially when you kick it into the 18-yard box. Before the start of the game, I communicate to my teammates my intentions when I am restarting the ball. They know to set up quickly so that I will pass the ball to them.

However, this can be easily overcome by the other team when a defender or the goalkeeper immediately starts barking out orders. This ensures that everyone on the defending team is in position to defend the corner kick no matter how quickly it is played into the box. It is incredibly demotivating, can halt your team's momentum, and often results in finger pointing when the other team scores what you may consider a "cheap" goal because your team was not paying attention.

Though the other team may view it as a cheap goal, it is great for your team because a goal is a goal. When a quick goal off a fast restart is scored against your team, it is mentally challenging to overcome. Communication builds chemistry, so establish before a game that there should be no mental breaks when your team is caught off guard during a restart. Also, consider having a player stand directly in front of the ball on set pieces to buy a few more seconds of time for their team to become organized.

As stated in the fourth book in the Understand Soccer Series, *Soccer Passing & Receiving*, **yell don't call**

and demand don't ask. If you are the leader in the backfield, yell out your orders with confidence. Demand that the players go to the correct positions, do not ask that they do it. Shouting with conviction will ensure your teammates follow your orders immediately. Defenders and the goalkeeper have the best view of the field and where everyone is positioned. So be a leader by directing people to where they will be most effective.

Additionally, considering that the other team is attempting to catch you off guard, be sure to return the favor. Turn their fast restart into a counterattack for your team since many of their players likely will have pushed up the field to support the restart. **When clearing the ball, either have a predetermined spot up one wing where a forward will be located or clear it in the space just past the defensive line of the opposing team.** The area just beyond the defensive line of the other team is very dangerous for them. A forward can run into this space to receive the ball and force the defenders to turn their backs to the direction they need to score. Do not clear the ball to the area in front of the defenders on the other team because they will just kick or head the ball back to begin another attack.

In conclusion, follow these simple guidelines to defend fast restarts:

1. Do not take a mental or physical break
2. Immediately yell out orders
3. Clear the ball to a predetermined spot or behind the other team's defensive line to start your team's fast break

Chapter 11

How to Shield the Ball

It is crucial that you protect the ball to ensure that you can distribute it to your teammates. The following chapter is an excerpt from the fourth book in the Understand Soccer Series, *Soccer Passing & Receiving*. To shield the ball appropriately as a defender, consider the following three things:

1. Have a low center of gravity
2. Spread your arms
3. Push the ball away from pressure

1. When shielding the ball with an opposing player behind you, **it is vital to have a lower center of gravity than the opponent who is reaching in for the ball.** A lower center of gravity will give you a solid foundation to make it nearly impossible for the other player to move you and take possession of the ball. Your center of gravity is how high your hips are from the ground, so within reason, bringing your hips down several inches or even a full foot will make it so you are more stable and more difficult to push off the ball. This positioning is similar to that of a quarter squat where you squat 1/4th of the way down. This position is optimal to shield the ball from the other team.

2. **Have your arms out.** Having your arms out means both extending at the shoulder and at the elbow to make your body and your arms as wide as possible. Though you are often taught from a young age that you are not supposed to have your elbows or even your arms up, the referees will hardly ever call you for having your arm raised, especially when you are shielding the ball from a player on the other team. Having your arms out and using them as leverage to make it more difficult for the opposition to steal the ball increases the chance you will effectively shield the ball and be able to pass it to a teammate. Having your arms out naturally makes you wider and therefore it will take longer for the opposing player to travel around your body and arms to steal the ball. Even if the opponent does, you can

take a touch away from them to buy you more time. Use the area on your forearm between your wrist and elbow to make contact and provide the best advantage while giving enough space between the ball and the defender.

3. When shielding a ball, it is important that you are not afraid to take a touch away from pressure. **A touch away from pressure will help generate some momentum and buy you more time to decide how you will pass the ball to a teammate.** If a player on the other team is coming to your right side behind you, then push the ball more towards the left and vice versa. Having the ball on the side away from the opposition allows you to keep your body entirely between the ball and the other team's player.

Obviously, your size and the size of your opponent does make a difference. If you are a 5'5" soccer player and you are going up against a 6'5" opponent, you will find that their leg length and natural strength will make it difficult for you to shield the ball. **If you are at a significant size disadvantage, avoid situations where you may be required to shield the ball.**

In conclusion, keep your center of gravity low by going a quarter of the way down into a squat. Spread your arms out at the shoulder and the elbow, so they are wide and away from you. Do not be afraid to move the ball away from pressure temporarily to ensure that you can shield the ball properly. Watch Philipp Lahm, the German National Team star and Bayern Munich player, for a great example of a small player who follows the concepts in this chapter to shield the ball effectively from his opponents.

Chapter 12

Clock Management

Soccer is a sport with a fixed amount of time. Unlike baseball, tennis, and golf, soccer is a sport that is both a competition against the other team and a race against the clock. Due to the fact that there is a set amount of time, being able to manage the clock is essential. Often, games will have a scoreboard, so all players, coaches, and spectators know precisely how much time is remaining. **If there is no scoreboard with the time, then a coach or two on your team should be using their own watch to ensure that they correctly manage the time remaining.** Let us discuss a few ways to control the clock as an additional way to prevent goals by the other team.

You should consider your team's style of play and the tactic the coach chooses, but oftentimes one of the worst things that a team can do is to go purely into a defensive mode if they score an early goal. The goal has just generated momentum for your team and switching to a defensive mindset limits your team's ability to provide a cushion of two or three goals. However, if your team has a great forward and a solid defense, then absolutely look for opportunities to counterattack, but avoid limiting your team's play style too early in the game. The longer you focus on defense early in a game, the more you become relaxed. This increases the chance that the opposing team will begin to close the passing lanes down and eventually intercept a pass in a position that can create a quick counterattack. Playing too defensively is a risk you will want to avoid.

I have a good friend and teammate named Toni Sinistaj that is always very ungenerous with restarts on the soccer field when his team is ahead. He does whatever he can to buy his team more time by taking longer to give the ball to the other team or making sure his team is in the position they need to be before giving the ball to the person taking the throw-in. **He does a great job to avoid placing his team and himself in a disadvantaged position when he has the power to do something about it.**

I always give him a hard time for doing this tactic anytime that I am on the other team in a practice, scrimmage, or pick-up game because I am trying to help my team win. However, I respect him and his strategy because it helps his team and is entirely within the rules. **However, avoid taking too long by doing this because you will receive a yellow card from the referee for a delay of game.** This seemingly petty tactic might not be received well by the other team, but remember you are playing a competitive sport and using clock management strategies can be the difference between winning and losing a game.

During the game, by promptly giving them the ball, you are letting them win a small battle. Do not retrieve the ball for the opposition because that will save them time and energy. Sure, allowing them to win these small battles in many situations will not be detrimental to your team and will not lead to goals. However, a few times a season, these situations turn into goals for the other team that is paying better attention and is ready to act appropriately. **This is also an excellent opportunity for your team to catch their breath if they have been running a lot.** Simply holding the ball a bit longer or dropping it to the ground so the opposition has to spend time collecting it, can buy your team some added physical and mental rest.

Next, if you are looking to kill time during the game, passing among the defenders and midfielders on your team is terrific. Granted, your team must have the talent to maintain possession. **Otherwise, in the last few minutes of the game, consider kicking the ball up the field or having one of your best players dribble the ball to the corner flag and attempt to prevent the other team from gaining possession.** Tactics like this may be considered a bit unsportsmanlike, but are certainly within the rules of the game and should be considered when your team is looking for any advantage to run out the clock for a win.

In summary, use appropriate clock management techniques when looking to sustain a lead in a game:

1. Avoid quickly giving the ball to the other team when it goes out of bounds. Make them use their energy to get the ball and give yourself time to be properly positioned.

2. Pass the ball extensively to tire the other team's forwards and midfielders (the players that will need the most energy towards the end of the game to score).

3. When in uncomfortable situations, kick the ball past the other team's defenders or run the ball to the corner flag to delay the other team from gaining possession.

Chapter 13

Defending in a 2v2

A 2v2 is a typical scenario that defenders will find themselves in during a game. Clearly, the best way to defend is to avoid unfavorable situations altogether. Cutting off passing lanes, being in the correct position, and having several players behind the ball (between the ball and their own net) will reduce the need to recover from a situation in a game where only a few players are involved. However, since this does not always happen, this chapter will be relevant to a 2v2 when you are in the defending third of the field, working to prevent the other team from scoring a goal. Consider the following things to increase your chances of successfully stopping the two attacking players:

1. Slow the forwards' momentum to allow teammates to hustle back
2. Bring both of the attackers as close together as possible
3. Focus on positioning based on which attacker has the ball

1. **Even if you and your defending teammate do not steal the ball immediately, you both will be considered successful if you can slow the attackers' progress up**

the field enough for your teammates to come back into position and help defend. Stalling the attacking player's momentum in 1v1s, 2v1s, and 2v2s makes it much easier to defend. Limiting their forward progress increases the chance that supporting teammates can hustle back into position to become additional defenders and it reduces the chance that the attacking players sprint by you. Again, placing your arms in the way of the attacking player, making yourself bigger by having your arms spread, and a moderately wide stance will go a long way in slowing the attackers' progress. In addition, having 2-3 yards of space between you and the defender with the ball (if you are covering that attacking player) will provide enough space to limit the effectiveness of a foot skill and an explosive push of the ball after the foot skill by the attacking player attempting to create space between you and them.

2. **Avoid allowing the forwards to create several yards of space between you and your teammate. Allowing too much space between you and your teammate enables more options for the attacking player with the ball and a greater chance of scoring.** Specifically, if they elect not to pass the ball but to dribble their defender instead, they will not have to beat the additional defender as well. Furthermore, if the attacking player with the ball decides to pass the ball, allowing the other attacking player to be farther from their teammate will increase the chance

of there being an open lane behind you, the defender. Keep in mind that a 2v2 is very situational. A 2v2 in your own third of the field differs greatly from a 2v2 when your opponent is not within striking distance.

If you and your teammate can move the two attackers closer together, then there is an increased chance for an opportunity for you and your teammate to dispossess the attackers. Having four feet swinging at the ball trying to poke it away, instead of just two feet, doubles your chance of success. To avoid being too close together, attackers will often run into space hoping to enable an easy pass from his or her teammate. **Often, a great attacking player will take their first two to three steps in the wrong direction** hoping you will begin to cut them off in their initial direction, which will provide space to run in the direction the attacker actually wants to go.

In the league match against the other Dylan of Next Level Training, mentioned previously in this book, there was one instance where I was defending him about 20 yards away from the net. His teammate on the opposite wing had the ball and I was following the rule of forcing him to his opposite foot (his right foot). However, to my surprise, after his initial two steps towards his dominant foot, he quickly cut and exploded towards his right and towards the ball. Unfortunately, this misleading run provided him enough space to travel a step or two past me. The worst part about this was that he was now at the penalty spot while I was sprinting to recover. Luckily, the attempted pass to the other Dylan from his teammate was blocked. Had it not been, his misleading run would have produced an easy shot on net because I did not stay 3-5 yards away from him while defending him when he did not have the ball. I was only about 2 yards away from him when he used his very misleading run.

3. 3-5 yards of space between you and the player without the ball decreases the chance that the attacker without the ball can make a quality run past you and be played the ball by their teammate. **Understand that if you are covering the player without the ball, you must be closer to the net than your teammate covering the attacking player with the ball.** There are two reasons to be positioned this way. First, if the ball is passed, you will have time to adjust your position and move closer to the player who now has the ball. However, if you are farther from the net than your teammate while guarding the player without the ball, you allow an easy passing lane for the player with the ball to take advantage of, which almost guarantees a shot on goal. Second, if the opponent your teammate is guarding dribbles past your teammate with the ball, you will be positioned properly to run over to provide help.

Defending a 2v2

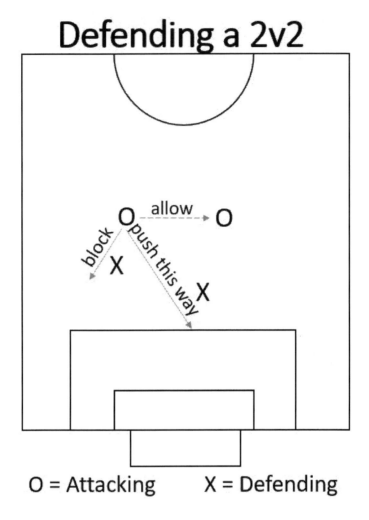

O = Attacking   X = Defending

Notice in the image that the defender closest to the player with the ball is 2-3 yards away. However, the defender covering the attacker without the ball is 3-5 yards from that player. If the ball were to be played horizontally to the other attacker, this is a good thing because the ball is not making any progress up the field and is only taking time to allow your teammates to hustle back to support. **If this should happen, then the defender now covering** the person without the ball should drop back, so they are 3-5 yards from the player without the ball. The defender of the player who just received the ball should now reduce the space between them to only 2-3 yards. In essence, the right defender in the image would shift forward if the ball were played to the attacker he was defending and the left defender would shift backward to provide more space between the attacking player and himself or herself.

Lastly, a key point to remember is to be explosive in these types of situations to avoid allowing the attacking players to catch you and your teammate flat-footed. By keeping pace with the player you are covering, you will increase the chance that your team prevents a goal. Therefore, be active and on your toes. Constantly talk to your teammate and tell them if you need them to adjust something and communicate your intentions as the play unfolds.

Chapter 14

Shot Blocking & Recovering when Dribbled Past

As a defender, shot blocking is a useful skill that allows you to frustrate the attacking players and dramatically change the speed and the direction of a shot. Understanding the chapter titled *Reading the Other Player's Foot Skills* will help you to maintain great positioning and increase your ability to block shots when the attacking player attempts to create space and shoot the ball. **However, when the attacker has space between you and them, you must prioritize blocking certain shots.**

Specifically, this means that you want to block every shot, but must **emphasize stopping the shots that will be difficult for your goalkeeper to save**. At higher levels, goalkeepers become increasingly difficult to beat. Shots that are powerful or well-placed are likely the only shots to give the shooter a chance at scoring. Therefore, when you are a few yards from the defender and looking to block their shot, know that your main priority is to block the shooting lane that would be most difficult for your goalkeeper to save.

When you watch some defenders blocking shots, you will notice that they position themselves directly between the goalie and the ball. This is deficient for two reasons. **First, this makes it difficult for the goalie to see the ball and react quickly enough to make a save if you cannot block the shot. Second, shots directly at the goalkeeper will nearly always be saved by the goalkeeper.**

Now, imagine the attacking player is striking the ball from the 18-yard box. Ideally, you want to be close enough to block all shots, but your priority should be preventing the ball from traveling to the far post, the spot in the net farthest from the goalkeeper. Shots to the far post are what a goalkeeper is worried about and not shots that are close to their body. **Think about it, when standing directly between the ball and the goalkeeper, a couple of yards away from the ball, you are preventing a shot from going towards a portion of the net that your goalie is also covering.**

Your team now has two players covering the same portion of the net but are still allowing a bent/curved shot to find its way around both of you to the uncovered far post. Therefore, set up in front of the attacker in a position that cuts off a shot to the far post from their preferred foot. **Also, when looking to block the shot, consider**

lowering one knee close to the ground to prevent the shooter from nutmegging you. Additionally, you will protect a wider area by preventing most shots on the ground because your leg is close to and parallel to the ground.

Another essential part of being a good defender is recovering when beaten by an attacking player. **Sadly, there will be times when the defender is defeated with a foot skill by the attacker.** Though it can be frustrating that you messed up, that should not affect the next actions you take. Often, other defenders will help cover and buy time for the beaten defender to regain correct positioning. However, you will not always have help and may have to recover on your own to avoid an easy breakaway for the other team. Clearly, speed plays a significant part and superior speed will allow a defender to catch up with the person dribbling the ball and use their body/shoulder to push the player off the ball or limit their ability to shoot.

Even if it does not seem like you will catch up, you must never give up on the play. There have been countless times that a defender mentally gave up on the play, only to see the attacking player make a mistake with their next touch or the goalkeeper make an excellent save but give up a rebound that the defender could have easily cleared had they been recovering correctly. Therefore, if you are beaten, begin running at full speed towards the nearest goalpost.

In order to beat you, it is likely that the attacking player had to use a skill that required them to change their direction and no longer be attacking directly towards the net. This change in the direction away from the net takes time and may provide you an opportunity to recover from your mistake. **While using your best judgment considering each situation is different, sprinting towards the near post will create the shortest distance for you to recover and will increase your chances of being able to block a shot.**

The defender often has less space to cover than the opposing player and can travel to cut off the angles for a shot, even if they cannot dispossess the attacker. **Most soccer players cannot time their shot correctly during a full sprint**, which gives you additional time as they slow a bit to strike the ball. Do not forget that just your presence may cause fear in the attacking player, forcing them to make a poor decision, rush their shot, or make a mistake. Defenders must always sprint to recover and only stop once their team has regained possession of the ball or the other team has scored.

To summarize, aim to block every shot, but make sure to primarily block the shots the goalkeeper will have a tough time saving. Furthermore, never give up as a defender, even if the attacker has beaten you. You have not been entirely beaten unless the ball is in the back of the net. Even if you do make a mistake and your team is scored on, keep your head held high because it takes multiple mistakes by several players on your team for a goal to be scored. Also, it takes many mistakes by each player over the course of an entire game for your team to lose, so wipe the momentary defeat out of your mind and continue to play as hard as you can.

Chapter 15

A Defender Receiving a Pass from Another Defender or the Goalkeeper

As a defender, you will often find yourself in high-pressure situations. Knowing what to do and how to perform it will take you from a good defender to a great defender.

1. Proper positioning
2. Scan and make a plan
3. Open up with the correct foot
4. Know your step over

1. When determining how to position yourself to receive a pass from the goalkeeper or another defender, consider the need to balance being wide enough with being able to recover if a mistake occurs. Generally, you want to have wide positioning when your team has the ball to allow the ball to work and force the other team to run. You want to be close together when the other team has the ball to avoid the other team easily passing through your team. Therefore, when your goalkeeper or defender has the ball, travel away from them to create space.

2. Then, scan the field before yelling for the ball. Avoid asking for the ball if you are under pressure. Scanning the field also allows you to determine what you should do next with the ball.

3. Next, use the foot of the direction you are attacking to play the ball. For example, you are the leftmost defender and are receiving a pass from the goalkeeper. In this situation, you would want to take an attacking touch using your left foot since you will be attacking to your left. Using your right foot would cross your feet and increase the chance of an inaccurate touch.

4. Lastly, realize that you do not have to win the game each time you receive the ball. Do not hesitate to pass the ball back to the person from whom you received it if you are not open and they still are. However, there will be certain situations where you have the ball with significant pressure and cannot pass it to another defender or the goalkeeper. In this instance, use a step over. **The step over is best used when your back is facing the direction you need to go. Never use it when you are attacking a player on the other team that is backpedaling.** Many soccer players mistakenly call a scissor a step over, but they are different. With a scissor, the foot closest to the ball would be the one that goes around the ball. With the step over, as you are standing

next to the ball, the leg farthest from the ball steps over the ball. Then, you bring your other leg around in order to plant your legs on the opposite side of the ball to push the ball away with the leg that initially started the step over. To perform the step over correctly, fully turn your shoulders in the direction you want the defender to believe you are traveling to fake them in the wrong direction.

A step over is an excellent way to fake out a defender when they are on your back. **The step over makes them believe that you are going in one direction, but you intentionally miss the ball**

completely, so that you can push it out and accelerate with speed in the other direction.

In summary, start by adequately positioning yourself so you can accurately scan the field. Receive the ball with the foot of the direction you are attacking and use your step over when you have a defender on your backside while you are facing the net as a defender. Understand that sometimes teammates will place you into a difficult situation. If you are ever uncertain about your best action, kicking the ball out of bounds to provide time for more defenders to travel behind the ball is acceptable too.

Chapter 16

Defending Tricks

This chapter reveals a few defending hacks that can make it easier to stop the other team from scoring. Little tricks are often as easy to do as they are not to do. Consider the following items as possible tactics to add to your game:

1. Call out the wrong time
2. How to pass back to the goalkeeper
3. Being nutmegged is okay
4. Defending as a forward

1. As the clock is running out, when you are playing in games that have a scoreboard and running clock, consider yelling out an incorrect amount of time remaining when the other team has the ball. **For example, if there are 15 seconds on the clock and they are close to your net, consider yelling out 6...5...4...3...2...1**. This trick often forces the other team's player to avoid making a quality pass in favor of taking a rushed shot that has little to no chance of going in. Since they are dribbling with the ball, they will believe the amount of time remaining that you are yelling out because looking at the clock will take extra time. Plus, when a player receives the ball near the end of the

half or near the end of the game, they will not be able to mentally account for the amount of time remaining and what they need to do with the ball. This trick works so well that when I have yelled out the incorrect time, I have had several opponents in the last few games take shots that are 30 or so yards from the net. These unrealistic shots made it easy for the goalkeeper to stop and prevented the other team from scoring.

2. When passing back to the goalkeeper, pass back across the frame of the net. **Specifically, pass the ball back so that even if the goalkeeper misses the ball, it will go out of bounds along the end line and not into the back of your net.** Even at the professional level, many goals have been scored because of a poor pass back or the goalkeeper mishandling the ball.

3. Many players make the nutmeg seem like one of the most important things in soccer. Many feel that you completely disrespected the other player and therefore are superior. In reality, a nutmeg is often a 50-50 chance because even if the ball goes through the defender's legs, there is a good chance that the dribbling player cannot recover the ball. Therefore, do not be concerned with being nutmegged. Naturally, it is not fun to be nutmegged, but being a good defender means preventing the other team from scoring. **Often, having your legs farther apart**

means there is a better chance you will be able to slow the attacking player because you are taking up more space on the field and are therefore harder to travel around. The nutmeg does not count if the other team cannot maintain possession of the ball.

4. When defending as a forward, determine the opposing team's weakest player on their back line and use nearly all your effort to take advantage of their weakest defender. Position yourself so it is most likely for the opposing team to play the ball to the back line's weakest player. **Once the weakest player receives the ball, you pounce and press that opponent heavily.** Other defenders may also be easy to take the ball from in certain situations, so be on the lookout, but know your most frequent chances will come from their worst defender, so pressure them hard!

These tips are easy to implement and will make defending easier for you and your team. From calling out a wrong time to correctly passing back to the keeper and being okay with being nutmegged to attacking the weakest link, look for opportunities to be the best defender you can be.

Chapter 17

Offside Trap, High Lines, & Low Lines

According to the Fédération Internationale de Football Association (FIFA), the governing body of soccer, a player is in an offside position if they are nearer to their opponents' goal line than both the ball and the second to last opponent. Offside occurs if at the same time the player is in an offside position, the ball is passed forward to him or her on the opposition's side of the pitch. **In simple terms, a player is offside when he or she receives the ball in a position between the last defender and the goal, while they are in the opposing team's half of the field.**

The offside trap consists of the defenders traveling higher up the field than one attacking player at the moment just before the ball is passed. When done correctly, the offside trap allows the defending team to win the ball back without having to intercept a pass, block a shot, or make a tackle. The offside trap is a high risk, high reward tactic for a soccer team. If it is done properly, the defense is awarded possession, but if there is even a small breakdown, a failed offside trap can lead to an easy goal.

Consider the following two necessities to implement the offside trap:

1. Generally, have a flat (straight) back line
2. Use a centerback that can read the game and communicate loudly

1. The defense must be ready to quickly and in unison or risk an opposing player being onside with few, if any, defenders between them and a shot on goal. This results in a relatively straight back line parallel to the goal line so that no one defender must move much farther than their teammates. It is okay for an outside defender to venture forward and be a part of the attack, but they must act as a unit with the other defensive backs when defending.

2. **The centerback must be able to analyze the play developing in front of them and decide when to use the trap.** The defender responsible for determining when to use the offside trap must know the location of their defending teammates and opposing forwards while understanding when the opponents are likely to kick the ball forward. The defender determining when to perform an offside trap should look for an attacking player that puts their head down before passing and an attacking player making a run up the field near the back line. Usually the

entire defense will take their cues from the centerback who is best at making these judgement calls.

Due to the need for a defensive line that works as a unit and good judgment by the centerback, **the offside trap is often used by experienced teams that have played together**. If a few steps forward would suddenly make the striker offside, then the centerback will move the defensive line up to win the free kick that is awarded because of the other team's offside. If the centerback believes the opponents will play the ball before the defense can step up, then they will probably tell his or her teammates to drop back and take a defensive position. Having fast defenders and especially fast centerbacks are helpful when using the offside trap, so they can recover if an attacking player remains onside.

The offside trap is simple to understand, but it is difficult to work consistently as one unit. The difficulty lies in coordinating, timing, and identifying those instances when the opposition is ready to play the ball. If the communication and timing of the defenders are not perfect, there is a high chance for an attacking player to have a breakaway. **Even if your team has perfected the offside trap, you will still run into a linesman or referee not calling an offside when there was one.** Furthermore, if the offside trap is overused, the opposing team will adapt their style to counter the offside trap.

To use the offside trap, your team likely cannot have a sweeper that is positioned deeper than the other defenders on the team. A sweeper will often ensure that the other team's player making a run will be onside when the ball is played. Because of this, the offside trap is best used with formations that do not use a sweeper.

As a defender, understanding how the offside trap can be defeated is important to help determine if it should be used in a specific instance. **First, if the opposing team has players who are good at using foot skills to travel past defenders, they can beat the first defender and force other defenders to cover in support.** The resulting disorganization by the defending team creates lanes to dribble in or make a pass to an onside teammate.

Second, a team may use short passes to break an offside trap. If the defending team does not apply enough pressure to the player with the ball quickly enough, the player who receives a short pass will have time to control the ball, look for a pass, and make a play to a nearby teammate.

Third, an offside trap is often ineffective against a team with a speedy striker. The striker will use their speed by running parallel to the defending line before the ball is played. At which point, the striker will explode past the defenders and have several chances a game to score against the offside trap.

The team using the offside trap may also use a high defensive line. **A high defensive line is a high risk (frequently allows breakaways) and high reward (many turnovers by the other team) style of play that involves a team pushing up the field to reduce the time the opposition has to dribble or pass.** Using a high defensive line reduces the size of the pitch by limiting the space and time when the opposition possesses the ball. Having a high defensive line will leave plenty of space behind the defense for speedsters on the other team to collect the ball and have few defenders to beat.

Defensive Line Positions when Defending

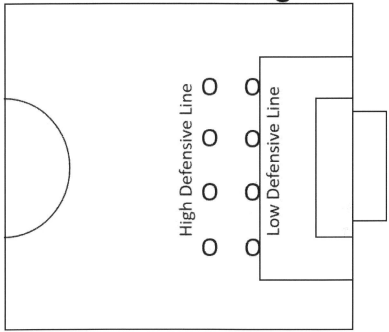

The **low defensive line, also known as the low block, is the opposite of the high defensive line. The low defensive line is a low risk (few goals against) and low reward (few goals for) style of defending.** The low defensive line is often used by teams with a good striker/center forward that can counterattack well or hold the ball effectively for supporting teammates. The low defensive line is frequently implemented with the 5-4-1 formation and involves the defending team attempting to keep the entire game in front of their defenders because they position themselves deep in their own zone. To read more about the 5-4-1 formation and a dozen or so other formations to determine which one is the best for your team, consider grabbing a copy of the seventh book in the Understand Soccer Series, *Soccer Coaching: A Step-by-Step Guide on How to Lead Your Players, Manage Parents, and Select the Best Formation.*

Chapter 18

An Example of a Defending Homework Assignment

"My ambition is always to get better and better" – Lionel Messi

Perform this homework in an open area. Ideas for when to do this are in the backyard during free time, before a game to warm up, and before the next practice. For those looking to develop their skills more quickly, practice this 3-4 times in the upcoming week. Have this done by the start of next week's practice.

Easy Rules to Remember for Defending:
1. P – Patience
2. A – Angled
3. T – Toes

Tips:
-Assume the attacker is right-footed until you observe otherwise.

-Push the attacker to their weak foot if they are in the middle of the field. Push them out of bounds if they are along a sideline.

-When the attacker turns their back to the net, be aggressive.

-Keep your arm/elbow up because it makes it easier to turn and makes you appear bigger.

-A good defender decides where the attacker travels.

Homework:

1. Run up to a ball and back pedal with angled form for 20 yards pushing the attacker to their left foot. Do this 4 times (focusing on an angled run to the ball).

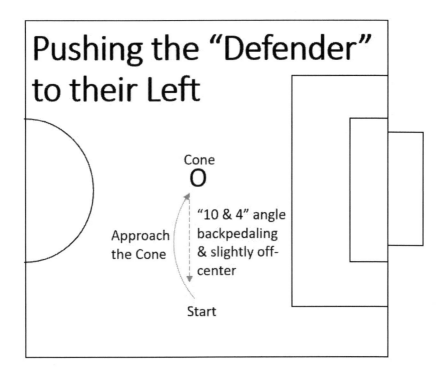

2. Run up to a ball and back pedal with angled form for 20 yards pushing the attacker to their right foot. Do this 4 times (focusing on an angled run to the ball).

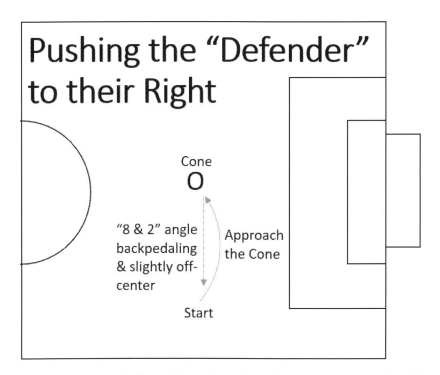

3. Run up to a ball and back pedal with angled form for 20 yards. Every 5 yards switch the direction you are pushing the attacker. Do this 4 times (focusing on an angled run to the ball).

Notes: Items 1-3 are working on approaching a cone (a defender) at an angle using a balanced stance with the arm closest to the defender raised. Ensure you are off-center to force the attacker in the direction you want them to travel, while having your feet at "8 & 2" or "10 & 4" to push the attacker to their right and left, respectively.

Bonus!

Wouldn't it be nice to have the steps in this book on an easy 1-page printout for you to take to the field? Well, here is your chance!

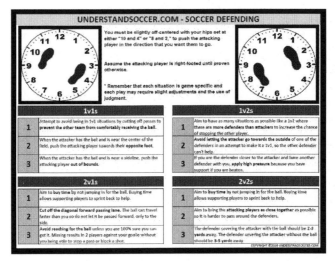

Go to this Link for an **Instant** 1-Page Printout: UnderstandSoccer.com/free-printout.

This FREE guide is simply a "Thank You" for purchasing this book. This 1-page printout will ensure that the knowledge you obtain from this book makes it to the field.

Free Book?

How would you like to obtain the next book in the series for free and receive it before anyone else?

Join the Soccer Squad Book Team today and receive your next book (and potentially future books) for FREE.

Signing up is easy and does not cost anything.

Check out this website for more information:

UnderstandSoccer.com/soccer-squad-book-team

Thank You for Reading!

Dear Reader,

I hope you enjoyed and learned from **Soccer Defending**. I truly enjoyed writing these steps and tips to ensure you improve your game, your team's game, or your child's game.

As an author, I love feedback. Candidly, you are the reason that I wrote this book and plan to write more. Therefore, tell me what you liked, what you loved, what can be improved, and even what you hated. I'd love to hear from you. Visit UnderstandSoccer.com and scroll to the bottom of the homepage to leave me a message in the contact section or email me at:

Dylan@UnderstandSoccer.com

Finally, I need to ask a favor. I'd love and truly appreciate a review.

As you likely know, reviews are a key part of my process to see whether you, the reader, enjoyed my book. The reviews allow me to write more books. You have the power to help make or break my book. Please take the 2 minutes needed to leave a review on Amazon.com at: https://www.amazon.com/gp/product-review/1949511111.

In gratitude,

Dylan Joseph

Glossary

4-4-2 Formation - Four defenders, four midfielders, and two forwards. A standard and balanced formation.

5-4-1 Formation ("Low Block") - Five defenders, four midfielders, and one forward. A defensive formation.

4-3-3 Formation - Four defenders, three midfielders, and three forwards. An offensive formation.

8 & 2 - The defensive position where your feet represent hands on a clock. Use this positioning when you want to push the attacking player to their right foot.

10 & 4 - The defensive position where your feet represent hands on a clock. Use this positioning when you want to push the attacking player to their left foot.

50-50 - When a ball is passed into pressure or cleared up the field and your teammate and a player on the opposing team each have an equal (50%) chance of taking possession of the soccer ball.

Attacking Touch - Pushing the ball into space with your first touch, which is the opposite of taking a touch where the ball stops underneath you (at your feet).

Back Line - The defenders on a soccer team forming the line in front of the goalkeeper.

Ball Hawk - Someone usually close to the ball, in the right place at the right time, and a person who specializes in scoring rebounds.

Ballistic/Dynamic Stretching - Form of active movement that is not about holding a stretch but taking your body through ranges of motion that warm you up for your workout or sport. For example, shaking out your arms and performing leg swings.

Bat - The bone (hardest portion) of your foot.

Behind the Ball - When a player is between the ball and the net.

Bent/Curved Shot - A shot that spins and curves as it goes towards the net. This shot is used when you need to shoot around defenders or goalkeepers. Though you use the bone of your foot to strike the ball instead of following through the ball with your entire body, you just follow through with your leg and cross your legs after shooting the ball.

Bicycle Kick ("Overhead Kick") - where the ball is above you and you jump up and kick the ball over your body while the ball is in the air.

Big 3 Foot Skills - The jab, la croqueta, and the shot fake.

Big 3 Formations - 4-4-2, 5-4-1, and 4-3-3 formations.

Block - Deflecting or stopping the shot of an opposing player.

Broom - In this book, it is the area on your foot towards your toes. There is space in your shoe between your toes where there is a lot more fabric and a lot less bone, which makes it a soft area on your foot, similar to the softness of a broom.

Champions League - The UEFA Champions League is an annual soccer competition involving the best of the best club teams from many of the professional leagues in Europe.

Chop - This is performed with the outside of your foot. The leg that is cutting the ball must step entirely past the ball.

Then, allow the ball to hit that leg/foot, which effectively stops the ball. Having the ball stop next to your foot enables the ball to be pushed in a different direction quickly.

Clearance - Kicking the ball up the field and out of pressure.

Counterattack ("Fast Break") - When the team defending gains possession of the ball and quickly travels up the field with the objective of taking a quick shot, so few of the other team's players can travel back to defend in time.

Crossbar Challenge - Played by one or more people where you attempt to hit the crossbar by shooting the ball from the 18-yard box.

Cruyff - Cut the ball, but leave yourself between the defender and the ball. In essence, you are cutting the ball behind your plant leg.

Cut - This is performed with the inside of your foot. The leg that is cutting the ball must step entirely past the ball. Then, allow the ball to hit that leg/foot, which effectively stops the ball. Having the ball stop next to your foot enables the ball to be pushed in a different direction quickly. Additionally, you may cut the ball so it is immediately moving in the direction you want to go.

Deliberate Practice - This form of practice is purposeful practice that knows where it is going and how to get there. It is guided by an understanding of what expert performers do to excel. For example, juggling with the tops of your feet towards the toes 30 times in a row to become better at settling the ball out of the air.

Driven Shot - A shot struck with the bone of your foot, where you follow through with your entire body without crossing your legs. This is the most powerful type of shot.

Finishing - The purpose of shooting, which is to score.

Flank - The right or left sides of the field closest to the sidelines.

Flick - Barely touching the ball to change the direction of the ball slightly for a teammate when a pass is being played to you.

Foundations - Passing the ball back and forth from one foot to the other using the inside of your feet.

Gegenpressing ("Counter-Pressing" or "6-Second Defense") - High pressure within the first six seconds of losing possession of the ball while the opponent is not set up properly to attack.

Habitual/Regular Practice - The most common form of practice where a person goes through the motions, repeating what they normally do, without being challenged or having a set goal. For example, practicing shooting from the penalty spot for fifth practice in a row.

Half-Volley - Striking the ball just after it hit the ground, but while the ball is still in the air.

Hyped - promote an idea or action intensively to emphasize its importance or benefits.

Interception - Stepping into a passing lane to dispossess the other team during a pass.

Jab Step ("Feint," "Body Feint," "Fake," "Fake and Take," or "Shoulder Drop") - When you pretend to push the ball in one direction, but purposely miss, then plant with the foot that you missed the ball with to push the ball in the other direction.

Jockeying - When defending, backpedaling to maintain a proper position in relation to the person attacking with the ball. When jockeying, the defender does not dive in for the ball. He or she waits for the ideal time to steal the ball or poke it away.

Jump Turn - Instead of pulling the ball back with the bottom of your foot, as you would do in the V pull back, stop the ball with the bottom of your foot as you jump past the ball, landing with both feet at the same time on the other side of the ball. Landing with both feet at the same time on the other side of the ball allows you to explode away in the direction from which you came.

Offside - When you pass the ball to a player on your team who is past the opposing team's last defender at the moment the kick is initiated. You cannot be offside on a throw-in or when you are on your own half of the field.

One-Time Shot - When a pass or cross is played to you and your first touch is a shot on net.

Opposite Foot - Your non-dominant foot. Out of your two feet, it is the one you are not as comfortable using.

Outside of the Foot Shot ("Trivela") - Shooting with the bone of your foot where your toe is pointed down and in. The ball makes contact with the outside portion/bone of your foot. This shot is useful because it is quicker than a driven shot, it can provide bend like a bent shot, and is more powerful than a pass shot.

Park the Bus - Often, when a team has a lead, a coach will tell all their players to come back and focus almost exclusively on defense to help protect the lead

Pass Fake - Faking a pass. Keep your form the same as when you pass, including: 1) Looking at a teammate before you do a pass fake 2) Raise your passing leg high enough behind your body, so that an opponent believes you are going to kick the ball.

Pass Shot ("Finesse Shot") - A shot on the net using the inside of your foot to increase your accuracy. However, land past the ball on the follow through to increase the shot's power, similar to a shot taken with the bone of your foot.

Passing Lane - An area on the field where a teammate can pass you the ball directly, while the ball remains on the ground.

Pitch - A soccer field.

Point-Man - Often a tall and strong center forward capable of winning 50-50 battles when the ball has been cleared up the field. This player's size and/or abilities help them to hold off the defenders and allow other teammates to join the attack and travel into passing lanes.

Purposeful Practice - Practice where you set specific goals for what you want to complete successfully. For example, I want to juggle the ball 30 times without letting it hit the ground.

Rainbow - When you place one foot in front of the ball and the laces of the other foot behind the ball. Pin the ball between your feet and flick the ball up behind your body and over your head.

Recovery - Intercepting a pass shortly after your team was dispossessed.

Roll ("Rollover") - Using the bottom of the toes of your foot, roll the ball parallel to the defender, crossing your feet when you plant. Then, bring your other foot around to uncross your feet and push the ball forward. The path the ball takes is the shape of an "L."

Sandwich Feedback Technique - Give a compliment, followed by giving feedback with an explanation ended with another compliment.

Self-Pass ("L," "Iniesta," or "La Croqueta") - Passing the ball from one foot to the other while running. Imagine you are doing a roll, but without your foot going on top of the ball. Instead, it is an inside of the foot pass from one foot and an inside of the foot push up the field with the other foot.

Set Piece ("Dead Ball") - A practiced plan used when the ball goes out of bounds or a foul is committed to put the ball back into play. The most common set pieces are throw-ins and free kicks.

Scissor - When the foot closest to the ball goes around the ball as you are attacking in a game. Emphasize turning your hips to fake the defender. To easily turn your hips, plant past the ball with your foot that is not going around the ball so that you can use the momentum of the moving ball to your advantage.

Shielding - Placing your body between the ball and the defender. With your back facing the defender and your arms wide, prevent him or her from traveling to the ball.

Shot Fake - Faking a shot. Make sure your form looks the same as when you shoot, including: 1) Looking at the goal before you do a shot fake 2) Arms out 3) Raise your shooting leg high enough behind your body, so it looks like you will shoot.

Square to your Teammate - Pointing your hips at a teammate.

Step On Step Out - To change direction, step on the ball with the bottom of your foot. Then, with the same foot that stepped on the ball, take another step to plant to the side of the ball, so that your other leg can come through and push the ball in a different direction.

Step Over - When you are next to the ball and you have your furthest leg from the ball step over the ball, so your entire body turns as if you are going in a completely different direction. The step over is best used along a sideline.

Sweeper - A defender that has no specific man-marking responsibilities and will often be situated behind their defending teammates to help "sweep up" any balls that travel through the defensive line.

Through Ball/Run - When a pass is played into the space in front of you, allowing you to continue your forward momentum.

Tiki-taka - high probability/short passing to help a team maintain considerable possession of the ball and frustrate the other team who is given as little as 15% time of possession.

Toe Poke/Toe Blow - Striking the ball with your big toe. The toe poke is the quickest shot, but often the most inaccurate shot.

Toe Taps - Start with the bottom of the toes of one foot on top of the ball and the other foot on the ground. Then, switch your feet so your other foot is now tapping the ball. Repeat back and forth using both feet.

Treble - When a club soccer team wins three trophies in a single season. A continental treble is earned by winning the club's national league competition, the national cup competition, and a continental trophy. A domestic treble is when a team wins three national competitions.

Competitions which comprise a single match do not count towards a treble.

UEFA Champions League - A tournament of qualifying teams in Europe held yearly to determine who is considered the world's best club team (the European Champion). Often considered one of the top two trophies that every soccer player dreams of winning (the other being the World Cup).

Upper 90 - Either of the top corners on a net (corners are 90 degrees).

V Pull Back - Pull the ball backward using the bottom of your foot. Then, use your other leg to push the ball and accelerate forward in the other direction, hence the "V" in the V pull back.

Volley - Striking the ball out of the air before it hits the ground.

Wall Passing ("1-2 Passing") - A wall pass is when you pass it to a teammate and they pass it back to you with one touch similar to if you were to pass a ball against a wall.

Acknowledgments

I would like to thank you, the reader. I am grateful to provide you value and to help continue your journey of becoming a better and more confident soccer player, soccer coach, or soccer parent. Honestly, I am happy to serve you and thank you so much for the opportunity to do so.

Also, I would like to thank my soccer mentor, Aaron Byrd, whose wisdom and soccer smarts have turned me into the player I am today. His guidance about this beautiful game has paved the way so that I can successfully pass this knowledge on to rising stars, coaches looking to improve their understanding of soccer, and caring parents! His training programs at Next Level Training are top-notch and highly recommended.

Many thanks,

Dylan Joseph

What's Next?

Each of the chapters in this book aims to increase the chance that you are able to prevent the other team from scoring. Implementing the tips, tricks, tweaks, and techniques you just read in this book will surely help you in achieving your dreams to become an outstanding soccer player. If you enjoyed the information within this book, please visit my website at UnderstandSoccer.com to let me know what you were most excited to read.

I aim to create a book on nearly every topic covered in the first book in the series *Soccer Training: A Step-by-Step Guide on 14 Topics for Intelligent Soccer Players, Coaches, and Parents* and would love for you to answer the **one question poll** at UnderstandSoccer.com/poll to help me determine what area of soccer you want to improve next. Your vote on the upcoming books in the series will help determine what book is to follow!

69202878R00069

Made in the USA
Columbia, SC
13 August 2019